THE KING & I

A LITTLE GALLERY OF ELVIS IMPERSONATORS

PHOTOGRAPHS BY KENT BARKER
TEXT BY KARIN PRITIKIN

CHRONICLE BOOKS

SAN FRANCISCO

Library of Congress Cataloging-in-Publication Data

Barker, Kent.
    The King and I : a little gallery of Elvis impersonators /
photographs by Kent Barker : text by Karin Pritikin.
        p. cm.
    ISBN 0-8118-0244-2
    1. Elvis Presley impersonators--Portraits. 2. United
States-Popular culture. I. Pritikin, Karin. II. Presley, Elvis.
1835-1977. III. Title.
ML88.P76B3   1992
782.42166'092--dc20   91-48082
                                                        CIP
                                                        MN

Printed in Hong Kong.

Distributed in Canada by Raincoast Books, 112 East
Third Ave., Vancouver, B.C. V5T 1C8

10 9 8 7 6 5 4 3 2 1

Chronicle Books
275 Fifth Street
San Francisco, CA 94103

This book could not have been accomplished without the impersonators who not only posed but gave a little of themselves to help us understand their work.

We would also like to thank:
Catherine Berry
David Stevenson
Sy Sajid for the background of Background
Solutions/Chicago

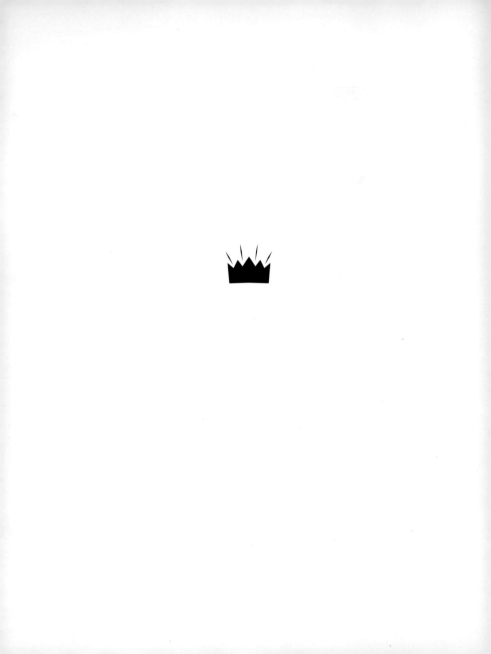

n June 1989, The Elvis Presley Impersonators Association of America held its first annual convention in Chicago—a three day conference with workshops, seminars, performances and award ceremonies. The portrait sittings and most of the interview sessions used in this book took place on site during this event.

The name Elvis is known around the world. Most of us can draw him with our eyes closed: the wavy pompadour; high forehead; straight nose and square chin. We can color in the picture without even thinking; the hair, black as night; burnished olive skin; dark fringed eyes, heavy lidded like a Renaissance madonna. And given just a hint of backbeat, we can do "The Show," the swiveling hips and curling lips; the haunting, taunting voice. He is a bona fide American icon, this Mississippi homeboy and Tennessee's adopted son. He lives in our collective consciousness along with Davy Crockett, Johnny Appleseed, Wyatt Earp, and Pecos Bill.

The fifties brought T.V. into our homes and with it a regal cavalcade of heroes, from buckskin-clad frontiersmen to champions of Catskills repartee to The King himself. Through this box in our living rooms, celebrities became accessible—our neighbors and friends. Elvis sang and spoke, and beckoned to us in a new, intimate way. He became, simultaneously, more influential and more real. Every night as we hunkered down with our coonskin caps and Mouska-Ears to watch the flickering screen, we dreamed of living enchanted lives, like our TV heroes. For some, this fantasy became a profession.

The dark, sensual, mysterious manchild in dungarees made girls across the nation swoon. Boys envied him and studied him. Six year old Kym Leonard saw in him the model of a perfect male:

"When I heard Elvis at age six, I fell in love; jumped around in my BVDs, totally captivated by the shake, rattle and roll—the whole package....To me, Elvis was suave, debonair, had all the right moves. He played music on the beach—but there were no musical outlets. His guitars never had cords on them—but they were loud, and twangy and cool."

And so, yearning to try on this strange persona somewhere between choirboy and biker, Kym copied him. In cities and in towns across the country, others followed suit.

The large, extended family Oscar Wilde grew up in was made up of diehard Elvis fans, and they indulged his fascination with delight:

"I had a little guitar, a little gold lame ́ suit...I worked on all those great movements—the jerky leg, the lip curl..."

Tony Roma, watching Elvis with his coterie of screaming girls, had a revelation that, somehow, even a shy polite guy could get attention, and thought "that's the life for me!"

These boys are grown men now, but the magic of that first encounter never waned. Today, all four are members of a unique club that inspires awe and, sometimes, disdain. They are Elvis Impersonators, just a few of the men and women who have appointed themselves keepers of The King's eternal flame. They have internalized the affect, memorized the moves and words so they may recreate The Show, weaving the illusion that Elvis is still here, in the flesh.

Some began performing while the King was alive, laboring to bring a moving, breathing Elvis to those of us who were too far away to touch the real thing. Others found their calling after he had died, giving us all the chance to relive a moment fixed in time. Jan Masserat first heard Elvis while vacationing as a young boy on the Italian Riviera. Though he spoke no English, he was

6

thrilled each time "Teddy Bear" came on the radio. Nonetheless, it was only later, after had had won acclaim as one of Switzerland's most popular singers, that he tried an Elvis act. The show received only lukewarm reviews, in part, he feels, because the concepts of nostalgia and Pop-culture were alien to the European mind:

"Americans like to celebrate their history and Elvis Presley is part of American history. The European mind is different; they see Elvis as the past and they're always looking to the future. They like the magic of being transported to Vegas in 1972, but they don't like to stay there long."

We visit passion plays and pageants to watch our history revealed. The creation is as important, in many ways, as the original. Seeing real men and women give shape to people and events that live only as memories, or entries in our books, leaves us feeling reassured, somehow, by a common lineage, a sense of place—a cultural continuum replete with rituals and rules. For a moment we become insiders, something that, save for a few exceptions, all of us want to be.

The Elvis transformation does double-duty, then. The player grafts himself into a grand and glamorous setting—feeling, in the process, a part of our cultural legacy. The spectators, too, relive a special moment they once experienced live or that they've seen before in pictures and on film. And so, for everyone involved, the sense of place and purpose is complete.

Louie Michael was thirteen years old when he booked his very first appearance—a performance at Red Foley's Ozark Mountain Jubilee:

"I called up all by myself and set it up with the guy. My parents didn't know about it. The night of the performance, I told them they'd have to drive me 'cause I was due to sing at 7 p.m. I didn't let any of the family in. I just went up there and got it over with."

7

For Doug Church, the pull came later. As a nine year old, he scoffed at his female cousins' infatuation with The King:

"...they were heavy into Elvis. I thought it was just a girl thing, just another singer they'd gone ga-ga over. I wasn't into music at that age, I was into adventure—Superman, stuff like that."

Then, in high school, Church's best friend was an Elvis fan:

"He pushed me to listen to him and I guess it just took. After school, I joined the Air Force and—with one fresh stripe on my sleeve—I took first place doing Elvis in a talent contest for the European command. I amassed 13 trophies during my tenure in the service—and just kept going from there."

Canadian Will Reeb sang along to Elvis while building model planes. His first appearance took place at a church youth festival before an audience of 2,000:

"I liked to pretend, I'd dress up like Batman or Superman. I like dressing up—it allows you to be somebody different for a while without losing yourself."

Learning of an upcoming Elvis fest, then fifteen-year-old Ed Hamilton paid $250 for a white jumpsuit. He felt an enormous thrill during that first show.

"I wasn't sure I was going to perform...I was backstage. Girls were swarming around me. It felt great. Then I went out and sang "C.C. Rider" and the crowd was with me all the way."

Spurred on by friends and families, these budding Elvises performed again. Soon, their phones began to ring, inquiries and bookings started pouring in—and their careers were born. With 600 songs to chose from, a repertoire that spanned rock-

and-roll and ballads, to country and religious fare, and a visual style that changed with every decade, there was more than enough material to inspire each and every imitator's own personal vision.

The cast of Elvises grows larger by the hour. Hobbyists hold day gigs and perform for free. Serious contenders eke out modest livings playing small town bars, county fairs, and charity bazaars. The lucky ones appear on television, cruise ships, and in traveling revues. And the stars headline their own shows in Vegas and Tahoe—dazzling spectacles with showgirls, singers, horns and strings.

For many Elvis entertainers, performing is a family enterprise. Mrs. Tony Roma schedules bookings. Julian Campo's aged Italian mother handstitches ruffled shirts. David Ehert plays keyboard and sings, while his daughter works behind the scenes. Don Sims' father appears as "hound dog" in his show:

"He dances with the audience...pulls people up on stage...and carries a basket full of stuffed dogs to give to fans."

Costume has an almost alchemical importance. Early impersonators made do with what they had around the house, or found in menswear shops. But now that The King is gone, there is a pomp and ceremony that surrounds the way they design and wear their outfits. While vintage fifties-style jackets are in fashion once again, seventies-style jumpsuits are impossible to find. Whole enterprises have sprung up to fill the void. Veteran impersonator, Frank Cannon, sews custom clothing for aspiring Elvises. B & K enterprises does a blockbuster business as a one-stop shop, selling do-it-yourself patterns, studs, fringe, boots, aviator shades, American Eagle belts, bell-bottomed suits, and capes.

But not all performers recreate Elvis' costumes to a "T," says impersonator Rusty Dee:

"Most guys duplicate Elvis' costumes; but every one of mine is different. The cut of the uniform is the same, but the decorations are unique. When I walk on the stage I'm in a world of my own making."

Some entertainers live full-time in their disguise, even though, as Ross Henderson of Melbourne will attest, there is a price to pay:

"Australians are real knockers. They're intolerant of anyone who is unusual or different. If I go into a place to buy cigarettes, I can usually count on someone starting a fight."

And then there are the performers like Kym Leonard, who, once the show is over, dismantle the routine completely:

"Back in the suitcase [Elvis] goes, with the hairspray and the jumpsuits—so it's all kept in its proper context."

Jan Masserat enjoys the fact that as a slight, balding, fair-skinned man no one would ever notice him after hours in a cafe, making his metamorphosis more complete when he gets into costume and backstage. Will Reeb is even more emphatic about the need to separate his personal and professional selves:

"We're called Elvis impersonators—that's what we are. The guys who try to be Elvis 24 hours a day become head-cases. Most of us are just trying to imitate him and his style...not fill his shoes."

Opinions may differ from performer to performer on costume, lifestyle, and acts, but one thing they all agree on is the special thrill they get when the lights dim and it's their turn to step out on stage.

When Doug Church performs, he mentally sketches out the persona:

"I see myself stepping into this outline. I turn my mind's eye inward and I create a mental picture of Elvis—of course, I keep my physical eye turned outward so I don't fall off the stage—and then I invite listeners into my realm."

Nigel Kingsley feels tremendous pressure as he prepares to go on:

"Right before you perform it is very stressful. People have big expectations—they're not waiting to see you, they're waiting to see Elvis, but they don't want you to come off as too close. They're quick to find fault."

Nevertheless, people, both young and old, flock to these shows to see The King recreated. As long as impersonators take to the stage, the cult of Elvis will continue. With every show, a crop of newer, younger fans comes to revel in His mystique. The first exposure many of these teenagers and kids have to The King may not come from films and specials on video, but from watching someone like Don Sims ply his trade:

"Kids are hooked by Elvis' cool sense of style. Recently we played a high school Christmas party and thought for a moment that his music might not go over—I figured they'd want AC/DC. But they were out on the dance floor the whole night with their pant-legs rolled up, gettin' down and having a great time."

After The Show, the kids go home and watch Elvis movies on TV. Some learn the words so they can sing along. Others like Paul Campione and Cory Heichel, pre-teen Elvis fans, study the movies so they can do The Show themselves.

To the men, women, and occasional children who have it in their hearts and minds to keep The King alive, there's much more to Elvis Aaron Presley than the music and the movies. To many he personified the American Dream. Steve Persson sees Elvis

11

as a man who stayed in touch with his humble beginnings:

"He was a lower income individual who fought his way through and stayed up at the top, but never forgot where he came from. He was decent to people, always helped them out...took care of his friends and gave to charity."

Will Reeb remembers Elvis as being accessible to everyone:

"[Elvis] wasn't standoffish. Even though he had bodyguards, he'd come down to the gates of Graceland and shake hands....he liked people. He knew that his fans were the ones that gave him everything he had."

Doug Church's Elvis was blessed with magnetism and charisma. Still, he attributes The King's extraordinary staying power to his voice—and reminds us that the impersonator's tribute is, above all, a form of entertainment:

"You could take all the jumpsuits belonging to every impersonator in the world and display them—put them on a wire and move it up and down to make them dance. But the real key is the voice. If you don't have a voice, there is no show."

Tony Roma agrees:

"There's never going to be another King....We are just his knights in shining armor."

FRANK IANAGGI

"Elvis' vibes come through me when I put on the suit. I feel like a different person. The suit is special; Ruth Crawford made it—she and her husband are my managers. But I'm new at this. I only have one suit—I'm like a newborn."

Boro, Ohio

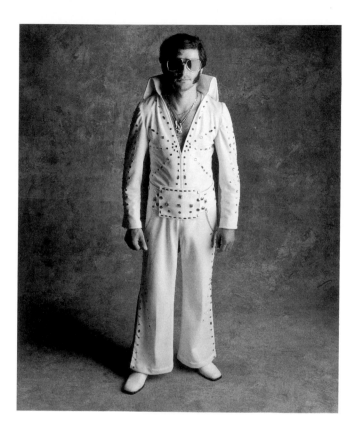

TONY ROMA

"I've never been to a convention of Elvis impersonators before. It's weird, because, before a show, I get in front of a mirror, put my suit on and psyche myself up. Seeing everyone else in their costumes— it's like looking through all kinds of mirrors."

Berwyn, Illinois

KEVIN MILLS

"I first heard Elvis when I was

eleven—I was really influenced by

the younger Elvis. Today, I have

five costume changes. But, unlike

most of the other guys, I start with

the fifties—Elvis at Sun Studio.

And I go all the way up through the

movie years."

Mt. Laurel, New Jersey

GABY SALAZAR

"I think Elvis had this amazing magic. Not only did he charm the women, but he also appealed to men and to masculinity. He was built...strong—at least up until the end. But he was sensitive, too. He could still cry and he was very polite and loyal. He knew how to give his fans what they wanted and still leave them hungry for more. I don't think anyone ever left an Elvis concert disappointed."

Berwyn, Illinois

OSCAR WILDE

"In my family, as I was growing up, my uncles, my mom, my dad, were all Elvis fans, I was surrounded by the Elvis music in the fifties and sixties. I wrote my own music when I was nine or ten, but I started with Elvis. He was my idol and I worked on all those great movements—the jerky leg...the lip curl...."

Waukegan, Illinois

Rusty Dee

"I'm a half breed—Irish and Indian. This necklace I wear, I designed—there's not another one anywhere in the world. Elvis' logo was TCB with a lightning bolt which means 'taking care of business'. My Indian name is Little Eagle which means 'free spirit'. The eagle stands for strength and freedom in this country. If you put it all together it says, 'with the strength of an eagle, we'll take care of business with tender loving care in just a heartbeat.'"

St. Petersburg, Florida

Danny Gonzolaz

"I try to incorporate other stuff into my routine. I even tried to sing some Buddy Holly, but it sounded like Elvis singing Buddy Holly. But I still go into my room and sing Beatles songs to myself."

Denver, Colorado

27

Paul Campione

"I have no brothers or sisters, just like Elvis. I like to play with Teenage Mutant Ninja Turtles and Nintendo, but I like singing and doing Elvis the best—and I like doing the ones that really cook! I was three years old when I heard Elvis. I thought, 'I want to imitate him.' I'm gonna do it until I'm forty. Not 'til I'm eighty, though. That's too old. I don't wanna do it until I have white hair."

Brooklyn, New York

JOE PAIGE

"When you're small, your folks always have something really nice they don't want you to touch. My father was a big Elvis fan when he was sixteen or seventeen, he had a lot of Elvis' records. He'd say, 'Don't touch those!,' which always made me want to get into them. I'd get my mother to put them on the Victrola we had and I'd sing along. And that's how I learned 'Blue Suede Shoes' at age three."

Berwyn, Illinois

WILL REEB

"When I was eleven or twelve, my mother had a portable 8-track player with an Elvis tape, which I took to my room. I would be doing stuff with my hands, building model kits—car models, airplane models—and singing as I went along, imitating the voice. Basically, Elvis taught me how to sing. I first imitated him at a church jubilee, with a band, singing for a crowd of 2,000. Since it was an annual thing, I began working on the costume, making it bigger and better each year."

Calgary, Alberta

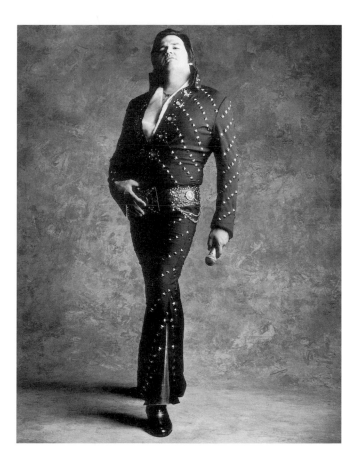

THE CAMPOS

Julian: "I eat Elvis...live Elvis...work Elvis...but most of all I pray with Elvis. My boy and I have a bond with Elvis that will never change. We're stuck together eternally...we have our own lives to live, but we're stuck with him and he's stuck with us. He's holding a hand to God and a hand to us."

Angelo: "We don't do [this] for us...we're here to serve God."

Chicago, Illinois

MIKE HOOVER

"I did Elvis stuff before he died; I had no idea it would become this big thing. I went to see some Elvis impersonators before my band really got rolling and I said, 'We could do that and maybe do it a little better.' So we got some suits and I figured we'd do it a couple of years. Before long, a couple years becomes five years...I don't even think about it anymore. I perform five nights a week and I'll do it 'til people stop listening."

Garrisonville, Virginia

NIGEL KINGSLEY

"In Europe, the competition isn't as fierce—but the love for Elvis isn't as strong. You can't make a living from it. I've done 600 shows in fourteen years, all throughout Europe: Germany, Switzerland, France, Italy, Czechoslovakia. But, even though we do tons of promotion, my best response is a surprise appearance, unannounced...."

Zurich, Switzerland

GARY MICHAELS

"I spent the first ten years of my life with my grandparents in Cherry Valley, Arkansas. My grandma used to sing me to sleep with gospel music. When kids up north were listening to the Beach Boys, we were listening to KMAG out of Fort Smith—Grand Ole Opry stars like Marty Robbins and Hank Snow. Once in a while when my grandmother wasn't around I'd mess with the dials and tune in the blues artists. I first heard Elvis on either the Dorsey Brothers program or a taping of the Louisiana Hayride. He knocked my socks off—all this energy was pouring right out of the speakers—and he'd blended the best of everything!"

Chicago, Illinois

LOUIE MICHAEL

"When I was thirteen, I heard about a talent show at the Red Foley's Ozark Mountain Jubilee. I called up, all by myself and set it up with the guy. My parents didn't know about it. The night of the performance I told them they'd have to drive me, 'cause I was due to sing at 7 p.m. I didn't let any of my family come in; I just went up there and got it over with. Later, the music teacher had me do Elvis music in the Christmas show. And from then on everyone called me Elvis around school and in town. When I played baseball, kids' parents would bring tapes of me singing and play them while I pitched."

Speed, Missouri

Ross Henderson

"I first heard Elvis on the radio at age eight, the year my father died. After that, I sort of styled my life after Elvis. My dream was always to do an Elvis show, but I had to wait until I was old enough. I wanted to do a proper one, so with the money from my plumbing—I had a very successful business—I put together a fifteen-piece show. Hired six of the best musicians money could buy. A guy to hand me my water and scarves. Three female vocalists. Assembled thirteen jumpsuits, $80,000 worth of sound equipment and lighting equipment and the guys to work it."

Brisbane, Australia

RICK ARDIGIANO

"People—my parents, my friends—

say I'm like a split personality;

when I'm up on stage I have a

totally different personality. I really

let go—it's my high."

Schaumberg, Illinois

GARY RAYE

"On my thirteenth birthday, I had

planned a tribute to Elvis show, one

of those neighborhood things. I

hadn't realized he had passed away

until someone told me, at my party.

It was a hell of a birthday present,

and a hard show to do, but I did it."

East Peoria, Illinois

CORY HEICHEL

"I broke my arm in fourth grade. I had to stay in bed; so I rented Elvis movies to watch. My Dad had been playing his tapes of Elvis a lot, and I became interested in him. His voice has so much power. It was amazing the way he came out on stage and had his own special moves. I decided to be Elvis for Halloween. Then, kids at school asked me to do it again at the school talent show and it spread like wildfire. I started getting one call after another..."

Westerville, Ohio

Robert Bradshaw

"I come from a religious family. I have a lot of roots like Elvis. My church is Pentecostal, Assemblies of God, same as Elvis. I have a lot of avid love for Elvis' gospel and the two groups that backed him up—The Jordanaires and The Imperials. But my family sees my admiration for Elvis as possession—they think I've turned him into some kind of God. So they don't give me any support for what I do. It's a real downfall."

Round Lake Beach, Illinois

DON SIMS

"My show has six performers and two technical guys...a great female vocalist...The whole band has been friends since high school...we have a fifteen-passenger maxi-van, and we tow our equipment behind us in a big trailer. We play private parties and holiday parties, nightclubs, county fairs, small town carnivals, and cruise ships. My family loves what I do. My dad's in the show. He dresses up like the hound dog... dances with the audience...carries a basket full of stuffed dogs."

Mt. Olive, Illinois

Rick Dunham

"I don't call myself an impersonator, because I don't look like Elvis. I call my show a tribute to Elvis, so people will know what they're going to get beforehand. I have to admit he was a very attractive man—it's hard for a guy to say that—but I envy him. I mean, who wouldn't want to look like that? But you're born with what you're born with and that's what you have to work with."

Dawson, Illinois

JAN MASSERAT

"I have loved Elvis since I first heard him on the radio, as I vacationed with my family on the beaches of Italy. Much later, I sang in Sweet People, a very popular European band. I was the one singer from Switzerland, sent to this big—European song contest in Jerusalem—I didn't win, ABBA did, with 'Waterloo.' When I came back, I started rehearsing with Johnny Holliday and Gene Vincent's pianist and a seven-piece group. After four years of practice, we did Elvis tributes all over Europe. I'm from Geneva...I'm not an American boy. I'm so far away from Vegas—just a little stone from the biggest mountain in the world—but I caught a little of the Elvis feeling."

Geneva, Switzerland

JAMIE COYNE

"At thirteen, all I listened to was vintage rock and roll—Carl Perkins, Johnny Cash, Elvis. When I started learning to sing and play, that's what I sounded like. It was just a natural progression from school talent shows to local talent shows to community events—car cruises, nursing homes, hospitals....Now I do fundraisers for charitable organizations, and though the money has started coming in, it's secondary; I'd do this for nothing."

Chicago, Illinois

Rick Marino

"There are only five American folk
heroes from modern times: Babe
Ruth. James Dean. Marilyn Monroe.
John Wayne. Elvis Presley. I don't
think there will be more; that's it.
They were special people. If you
look at all their backgrounds, with
the exception of John Wayne, they
were all troubled... interesting... self-
made people."

Jax, Florida

TRAVIS JAMES

"I do this full-time—no day gig—
and I've been doing it for sixteen-
plus years. Elvis was everywhere in
the house. My dad was a musician;
he had a rock-and-roll band and—
in his vocal style—impersonated
Elvis. So, since your dad is
supposed to be your hero, I just
followed in his footsteps. Now I do
really big shows—I've performed
with the Jordanaires and toured
Japan. And my folks are really
pleased that I do this...."

Hammond, Indiana

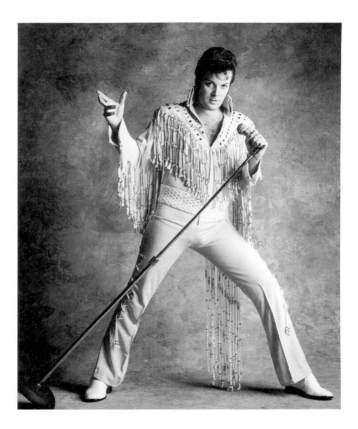

STEVE PERSSON

"My mom makes my suits. For the first jumpsuit, she made up her own pattern...I looked kind of bowlegged, like John Wayne. Today, she can make the real thing—we've both come a long way. It's hard to find all the things you need, though. The white leather boots have to be special ordered from Florsheim. The studs come from B&K Enterprises; they make a lot of the special jumpsuits. But, just to find things—like a necklace that looks like something he'd have worn—you really have to keep an eye out. And I wish they'd make better gold glasses—once you sweat, the gold comes off. The last pair had pink plastic underneath!"

Belvedere, Illinois

JULIAN CAMPO

"I have had contact with Elvis several times spiritually—he helps me to write songs. He told me, 'I'll never leave you, I'll always be with you. You got a lot to learn but you stick with me and we'll go all the way to the top.' He gives me guidance. I just pour his spirit into my body."

Chicago, Illinois

DAVE CARLSON

"I created the business because I'm one of the over-twenty-year veterans. People in the early seventies would drive fifty or a hundred miles to see an Elvis impersonator. But today it's not a big event anymore, it's something that's almost laughed at. I get treated almost as well as I imagine Elvis was treated. You know, the crying, the weeping, the screaming. People want to grow up and be like us. Elvis had such magnetism and such power, it doesn't matter if you're an imitation."

Oak Forest, Illinois

Nazar Sayegh

"Let me be honest with you, a lot of the people in the medical profession know about me. I've been interviewed by the American Medical Association, different journals, etc. I tried to keep it a secret for a long time. In the hospital I look completely different. I have a moustache on and I have short hair and a lab coat."

Yonkers, New York

JEROME MARLON

"I sang along with his records for so many years that I started to sound like him and I started making tapes to fool people. Today I do it for a living. I toured Russia last summer as a goodwill ambassador to the United States. The people would come up to me with pictures of Elvis and want me to autograph them."

Manteno, Illinois

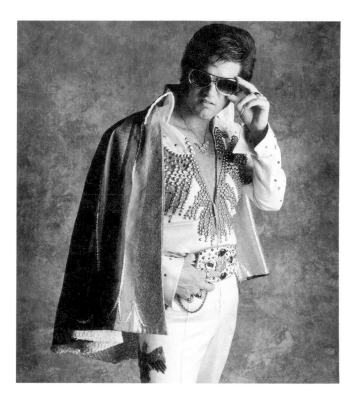

Johnny DeRose

"I keep thinking, is it going to go away? But I've been doing it for sixteen years now and there is no stopping it. I'm booked all the way into next year already."

Pembroke Pines, Florida

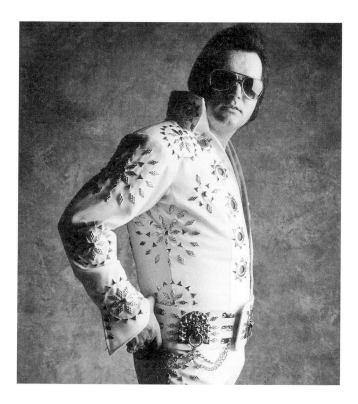

CLAY SMITH

"It was when I saw Johnny Rusk

impersonate Elvis that I decided to

become an impersonator myself.

I've performed with the Jordanaires

[Elvis' former band] in Memphis and I

have won two world impersonator

titles."

Memphis, Tennessee

BOB McVAY

"I was nine years old when Elvis first came out. I saw him on the Ed Sullivan show and after that I used to sit by the radio and try to imitate him. When I was in grade school they used to call me Elvis. My first show was for my twenty-fifth high school reunion. I was forty-two-years old and weighed 255 lbs. After that I was hooked."

Marion, Indiana

Robert Dye

"The only thing I really can't stand

in this world are people who make

a mockery of Elvis."

Crest Hill, Illinois

FRANK CANNON

"I was enthused about the way this Elvis guy affected women and I thought it would be nice to be a part of that, so I just started singin'. I really don't get into a lot of the moves that Elvis did, but I sing the song and I play the parts and I keep a part of me in there too."

St. Petersburg, Florida

JANICE WAITE

"There aren't too many female impersonators of Elvis, but at home in England he's not the only impersonation I do. I love rock and roll, that's why I love to do Elvis. I like to move the way he moved ."

Hertfordshire, England

Ricky Lee Shattuck

"When I first sing most people feel that I must be lip-synching. But when I cut the tape with the music on it everybody is blown away. I do sound like Elvis. I'm proud of that."

Woodridge, Illinois

JOHN ROSSI

"I believe that in order to do a good impersonation you have to interpret in a way that reflects the way you see Elvis. I see Elvis differently than others do and I think that my performance expresses that."

Wood Dale, Illinois

KENT BARKER

"I heard a lot of stories as I worked on this project, the best was as follows. I asked one of the impersonators if he had ever felt strange wearing the jumpsuit, gold chains, etc. Only once, he replied. Seems he was on his way to a gig in New York City and was unknowingly dropped off at the wrong hotel. He hopped out and proceeded into the banquet room where he believed he was supposed to go. As he opened the door and walked in, there was a hush as all eyes turned to him. Slowly, it dawned on him that everyone sort of looked alike...and then it hit him. He had walked smack dab into the middle of a Barry Manilow Impersonators convention."

Sante Fe, New Mexico

FRANK IANAGGI

"No impersonator could beat

Elvis...they're just out there singing

a memory."

Boro, Ohio